# catcalendar cats

# catcalendar cats

## THE COMPLETE COLLECTION
## WITH AN INTRODUCTION BY B. KLIBAN

WORKMAN PUBLISHING, NEW YORK

*Library of Congress Cataloging in Publication Data*

Kliban, B.
B. Kliban's catcalendar cats.
1. Cats — Caricatures and cartoons. 2. American wit
and humor, Pictorial. I. Title. II. Title: Catcalendar
cats.
NC1429.K58A4   1981   741.5'973   80-54619
ISBN 0-89480-169-4   AACR2

Cover and book design: Florence Cassen Mayers

Manufactured in the United States of America
First printing September 1981
10 9 8 7 6 5 4 3 2 1

Workman Publishing Company, Inc.
1 West 39 Street
New York, New York 10018

This book is dedicated to NokoMarie, Norton, Nitty, Burton Rustle, Judy, Kalia, Sarah, Toni and Michelle, all pussycats.

# Cats

As far as I know, cats were invented a few hundred years ago by some Egyptians, who noticed that they had the word 'cat' (or 'qat') in their language without anything to stick it on. The invention of cats (qats) filled in the gap nicely and the cat was off to a running start, as it were.

The cat would have remained just sort of a Teddy-Type animal had it not been for the addition of tiny fangs and claws around the time of the Civil War, on the same principle that a handful of jalapeños will perk up the morning oatmeal, or at least help it to catch mice.

After their perfection in 1935 (fatter tails, more ears) they rapidly became an important factor in the growth of the cat food industry, a mainstay of our western democratic culture.

An interesting fact about cats is that they will absolutely not do anything they don't want to, unlike us and dogs.

Now consider this chart of cat advantages—

| | DOG | FISH | BIRD | FRUIT | CAT |
|---|---|---|---|---|---|
| MEOWING | | | | | ✓ |
| CLIMBING | | ✓ | | | ✓ |
| PURRING | | | | | ✓ |
| CATCHING BUGS | | | ✓ | | ✓ |
| WASHING FACE | ✓ | | | | ✓ |
| NON-BARKING | | | | | ✓ |

I hope this has helped you to appreciate and understand qats a little more, so the next time you run into one, let him make you take him to lunch

BKliban
June 1981

# 1977

JANUARY

 FEBRUARY

MARCH

APRIL

MAY

JUNE

JULY

AUGUST

SEPTEMBER

OCTOBER

NOVEMBER

DECEMBER

# 1978

JANUARY

 FEBRUARY

MARCH

APRIL

MAY

JUNE

JULY

AUGUST

SEPTEMBER

OCTOBER

NOVEMBER

DECEMBER

# 1979

JANUARY

FEBRUARY

MARCH

APRIL

MAY

JUNE 1979

JULY

AUGUST

SEPTEMBER

OCTOBER

NOVEMBER

# DECEMBER

1980

 JANUARY

FEBRUARY

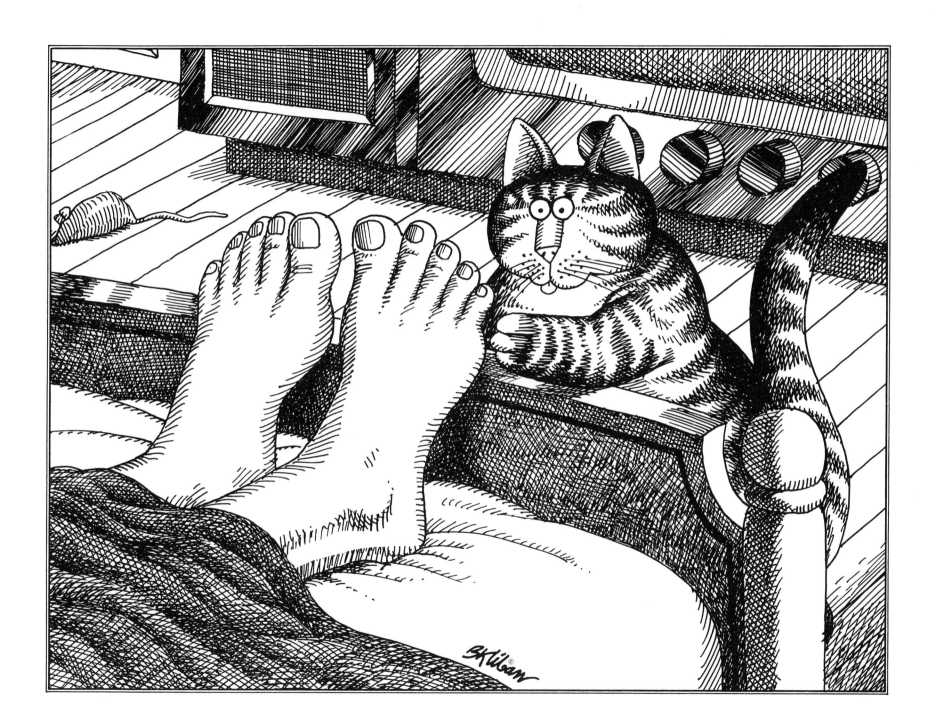

MARCH

APRIL

MAY

 JUNE

JULY

AUGUST

SEPTEMBER

OCTOBER

NOVEMBER

DECEMBER

# 1981

JANUARY

FEBRUARY

MARCH

APRIL

MAY

JUNE

JULY

AUGUST

 SEPTEMBER

OCTOBER

NOVEMBER

DECEMBER